# Ponder Awhile

# Ponder Awhile

## Message From The Light

**MOHIT K. MISRA**

Anecdote
Publishing House
*For the love of quality reading!*

**Anecdote Publishing House**
2nd Floor 2/15 Lane no. 2 Ansari Road,
Daryaganj-110002

Published by Anecdote Publishing House
Copyright © Mohit K Misra

Updated Edition 2024

ISBN 978-81-963155-7-3

MRP ₹ 199

All Rights Reserved.
No part of this publication may be reproduced, stored in a retrieval system, or transmitted in any form, or by any means—electronic, mechanical, photocopying, recording or otherwise—without the prior permission of the publisher. Opinions expressed in it are the author's own. The publisher is in no way responsible for these.

Book Promoted and Marketed by Champ Readers Pvt. Ltd.
Edited by Mansi Narula Kashyap
Cover design by Rishikumar Thakur
Layout by Graphic Tailor
Printed by Thomson Press (India) Ltd, New Delhi

Award Winning Finalist "USA Book News" Spirituality-General 2009.
Top 100 Customer Recommended Religion and Spirituality
"eBook Mall" 2009.

Ranked 1 in Religious and Spiritual eBooks "Franklin" 2010/2011.

"Best Book Buys" Ranked 1 in Poetry Books 2011.

Ranked Top 10 Poetry, Top 10 Body, Mind and Spirit and Top 10 Philosophy - Religious Books
2012 and 2013.

"I found that this book did make me stop and ponder for a while. It is like the calm in the eye of the storm. I found reading it a kind of literary meditation. It is thoughtfull, intelligent and uplifting, not only do I recommend it, I prescribe it. Trust me, I'm a doctor."

— **Benjamin Zephaniah (*The Times* list of Britain's top 50 post-war writers)**

"God Consciousness -
… I can confidently say the poems of Mohit. K. Misra are based on his experience of enlightenment and not from the learning gained from secondary sources … I strongly recommend to any 'seeker of truth' reading these poems to reading any religious book on this earth!"

— **Dr. Sunil Gopalchandra Samanta (New York, USA)**

"Garland of poems sensitizing deep thoughts in worldly reality. The sifting thoughts and emotions seeking out subtle nuances is a work of great mind … sustained by deep courage, commitment, daring and restraint. It is possible only by people who love and care for people. It is with a deep sense of fulfillment and urge to read again."

— **Anup Kumar Burman (Blue Cross Labs, Goa, India)**

Have a spiritual breakfast now!
"Pondering and wondering on the nature of man and God - One with a thousand questions and the other with a thousand names and answers - This young poet reminds one of Khalil Gibran with a touch of Tagore. We are sure that his delicious *Ponder Awhile* will give to the seeker of truth a longing for it and a taste of who we really are."

**– Raymond Gallaz (Reiki Master in Geneva, Switzerland)**

"A Brilliant Spiritual Work -
Some of the most poignant prose I have come across, relating to all aspects of religion and spirituality through harmony and unity of purpose. Mohit, crystallises all the main themes of life and its transition into beautiful and simple language... Really it is a very useful tool, when trying to understand these deep and often seemingly complex questions."

**– Peter Boaz Jones (Pete Author of *A New Millennium*)**

"Wonderful poems from *Ponder Awhile* -
I enjoy reading Mohit's poems. He has a tendency to rhyme and synchronise our everyday living circumstances with the divine. And some of them are philosophical indeed and make sense to the public at large."

**– E. Martin (Las Vegas, NV, USA)**

"This book is full of diamonds."
— **Swami Atmanand Vishnu**
**Pune, India)**

"A masterpiece one must have."
— **Vishal Lamba**

"In this series of autobiographical rhymes in innocence, earnestness and integrity of spirit is very touching. One would hope to hear more from this author."
— **Sona Singh (Artist, lecturer and tarot teacher for nearly fifty years)**

"A sneak peek into your soul -
This book took me for a journey which answered my question in such a way, that now I doubt if I ever had it! Every word selected and woven into sentences brings in soulful reflection. A must read for every soul searching individual."
— **Nabomita Mazumdar**

"I read the book and I like it very much. It touches the truth with your heart and soul and makes you very happy. One of the best books I have ever read. You also should read it!"
— **Peter Rueckert (Reiki Master, Yoga Teacher and NLP Master hypnotist)**

"A Navigating Officer in the Merchant Navy. Entering into a state of *Samadhi*, this author from Bombay intends to lead his readers into a spiritual experience."
**– Bruce Cook, Ph.D.**

"Wonderful book of poetry! He has some very interesting thoughts on light and death and I thoroughly enjoyed reading it."
**– Carol Langstroth (Manager, Mind Fog Reviews)**

"Best I ever read -
*Ponder Awhile* made me stop and ponder for a while. All poems are so beautifully written in simple manner yet they have so much deeper meanings in them. Some poems made me laugh and some made me cry also :) I thoroughly enjoyed reading it. Must read for all … it has got many answers to your life queries."
**– Reeta Mishra**

# Acknowledgements

Mr. Shailendranath Misra, Mrs. Preeti Misra,
Mrs. Phillomina Pervez, Mr. Keki Prevez, Dr. Naozer
Kavarana and Mr. AnilPrem Sharma

For their kindheartedness and love:

Minoo, Sameer, Joydip, Ameet, Vikram, Paso, Namit,
Akbar, Amish, Vibhu, Sheriar, Amar, Rabi, Niranjan,
Suhas, Adrian, Monty, Nitin, laxman, Manoj, Ranju,
Fuad, Yusuf, Prashant, Sabby, Monisha, Millie, Nawaz,
Ella, Tisha, Silvia and Meenal.

To all my relatives:

Deanne, Jasmine, Mehernosh, Percy, Kaizad, Adil,
Sanober, Shernaz, Amit, Rashmi,
Ira, Anita, Devesh, etc.

Miss. Hallegua, Cathedral and John Connon (Mumbai)

To You, To the Saints,

To God,

Special thanks to Shirdi Sai Baba.

*Ponder Awhile* has left me in deep contemplation.

Mohit expresses himself from the language of the heart, through the forces of nature. In his poetic compilation, psychology, science and mysticism become one with the power of Consciousness.

As an artist, I would like to salute this sensitive soul from the bottom of my heart.

**– Rashme Hegde Gopi**

In my mid-twenties, I was working in the Merchant Navy as a Navigating Officer. I believed myself to be very practical and logical, and didn't believe in the existence of God.

From a very young age, I would experiment with one pointed concentration in order to improve my concentration. It so happened that during a voyage from South Africa to South America, while practicing in the Atlantic Ocean, I entered into a state of *Samadhi* or gained enlightenment.

This experience altered my way of thinking drastically, as I believed God was a myth and death was the end of everything.

This was followed by various spiritual experiences, which led to absolute confusion as well as understanding. Reading the works of enlightened ones gave me solace and with time, I was given the signs by the Universe or God to write, to become a poet and share knowledge of God or knowledge of the Light. Hailing from a family of priests, my father's side being Hindu-Brahmins (the enlightened ones who settled by the river Ganges) and my maternal grandfather, a Parsee priest, I understood this was the reason I am here on this planet right now. Since spiritual books often possess profound depth and meaning, I aimed at writing with simplicity and have tried to get the greatest clarity possible so this knowledge can reach out to all. God and enlightenment are so misunderstood by most and I hope to clear people's misconceptions as well as doubts. There is only one God and all religions refer to God as the Light via different names. The main aim of my work is to unite all the religions.

Knowledge leads to understanding, which leads to peace and love, the source and basic fabric of this Universe or of God.

**–Mohit. K. Misra**

"Behold but one in all things, it is the second that leads you astray."

*– Sant Kabir*

"I am thy shield and thy exceedingly great reward."

*– The Holy Bible*

The first law of dynamics states that energy can neither be created nor be destroyed. So, what happens to that energy, that thing which animates the body at the moment of death?

"When we finally come to our senses, we never return to this material world, this painful playground we mistakenly call home."

*–The Bhagavad Gita*

"Unto Allah is your return and he is able to do all things."

*– The Holy Quran*

"Live and let Live."

*– Mahavira*

# Content

| | |
|---|---|
| Truth | 1 |
| Mother Earth | 3 |
| Friends | 4 |
| Time | 5 |
| Girls | 6 |
| Sea | 7 |
| Religions | 8 |
| Reason | 10 |
| Tapasya | 12 |
| Shoot The Goal | 13 |
| Magic | 15 |
| Trance | 16 |
| Mom | 18 |
| Tree | 19 |
| What | 20 |
| Charity | 22 |

| | |
|---|---|
| Peace | 24 |
| Win Some Lose Some | 25 |
| God Knows | 27 |
| Dream | 29 |
| Alone | 31 |
| Once Again | 33 |
| Gone Mad | 34 |
| Intoxication | 35 |
| Married To The Light | 36 |
| Infinity | 38 |
| My Second Father – Dr. Naozer Kavarana | 40 |
| Anil Prem Sharma | 42 |
| Confusion | 43 |
| Sameer S. Shetty | 44 |
| God | 45 |
| The Ultimate Plan | 47 |
| The Now | 48 |
| Lady | 49 |
| Tossed | 50 |
| Eternity | 51 |

| | |
|---|---:|
| Life | 52 |
| The Master | 54 |
| Desperate For Attention | 56 |
| Do Right | 58 |
| Focus | 59 |
| Curiosity | 61 |
| Ungrateful | 62 |
| Youth | 63 |
| The Human | 65 |
| Trespassing | 67 |
| Strange | 69 |
| Death | 70 |
| | |
| *Glossary* | *73* |

# Truth

Brahma, Allah, Jehovah, Vishnu, Ahuramazda,
Shiva …
What's in a name?
A way to identify the same,
Geography, language is mainly to blame.

Your glory is such,
Man asks for too much.

Meditation or one-pointed concentration is the key,
But, who says there is no fee?

Day to dawn makes no sense,
What does! We call nonsense.

Who am I and why am I here?
Has just become my greatest fear.

Is justice to be done with the strength in my hands?
Or, by sweet words maybe written in the sands?

When will you set me free?
So that I can be with thee.

How am I to live in bliss?
When I stop myself from giving all a kiss?

Why do I write I do not know?
It is only ink on paper to show.

# Mother Earth

Mother Earth actually looks after me,
She neither expects nor charges a fee.

Every year fresh fruits she provides to eat,
For those fruits, one another man will beat.

So much water is there for us all,
For water it often becomes an ugly brawl.

A tiny insect on Her I am,
Feeding me with her assorted jam.

Man keeps beating her with his big bombs,
When will he realise that She is alive and that it is wrong?

Her, we must begin to appreciate,
Immediately, before it gets too late.

From our puny race She will defend herself,
You are just begging Her to annihilate yourself.

# Friends

Friends come and go as they please,
True friends are rare indeed,
The ones that show up when you are in need.

The rest are all acquaintances to say,
In order to make time pass away.

The ones that last,
We have had a good past,
All in this play in which we are cast.

You should get to know yourself,
Man's best friend is himself.

We should learn from the mistakes we make,
But we foolishly keep going for a retake.

Another day, good morning hell,
What lessons for today, I cannot tell.

# Time

Time actually seems to fly,
How fast has my life gone by.

Trying to make sense of things,
Time was made for order to bring.

The seconds tick, the minutes past,
Even the hour, day, month and year is not meant to last.

In this dimension time cannot be stopped,
In another dimension time is automatically dropped.

The master plan must be perfectly timed,
So the truth by us can be tapped and mined.

# Girls

Why in the world did you make girls,
Some so beautiful, my head I have to twirl?

Does she know in me she creates a sensation?
I have started thinking of the word creation.

So many around so gorgeous,
My mind seems frivolous.

How the hell am I supposed to just stay with one?
I want all the pretty ones as they come,
Then these things I want none.

I know they are all but your form,
The rose comes with the thorn.

Show me the path, I pray to you,
So, I know what to do.

# Sea

The sea is so very powerful,
She eats the metal of the ship's hull.

Her fury is so great,
Her beauty you simply can't hate.

Endless and huge she seems,
Drop by drop together teams.

You want to jump right into her,
Hypnotising she; can erase your fear.

She not once demanded my respect,
I gave it gladly with no regret.

Her depth such deep silence,
Contemplating, penance.

How much magic do you hold?
With you in the end I will mold.

# Religions

The entire Buddhist monk's life is, but a preparation,
For his Death Point or moment of separation.

The Jains have *Santhara*,
Quitting life consciously to join with the *Paramatma*.

Hindus go into *Samadhi*,
Where there is no Congress, Shiv Sena, BJP or Samajwadi.

The Christian merges with the Holy Spirit,
Peace no more desperate.

The Sufi mystic to become one,
Dances, twirls, prays, trances to get the job done.

*Aghora* means Illumined with Light,
Longing for Shiva in whom they delight.

Shamanism or the Art of Ecstasy,
The ultimate being one with the super-entity.

There is no need to change your faith,
And on your old religion lay a wreath.

# Reason

I am in control of parts of my body.

Something else or some other I, controls the rest,
like my breath, heartbeat, veins, etc.

Am I really in control? I say No.
So, what is controlling everything besides me?

The same force or entity or power controls.
I have never been in control.
At the same time, I must have been in control.

We have taken over the planet, bullied other animals.

Are we abusing our power or does
the game of the survival of the
fittest carry on?
I say we are abusing our power.

This ridiculous precision of revolution, rotation of the
earth, moon and planets for thousands
and thousands of years.
Something, if not someone has assembled all this.
Based on this accuracy man invented time.

What has the capacity to play with or organise such
gigantic spheres?
Our solar system is just a small part of this cosmos.
God knows for how many generations this
is all going on.

We are connected together as the human species,
Deeper than that blood relationship and friendship.
Deeper the light, love, super intelligent, super entity.
What we term as God.

# Tapasya

My twin sister's name is Tapasya,
She is also a part of the *Maya*.

Shanaya and Talisa; her twin daughter's names,
An extension of her, they are all the same.

What attitude for a two year old child,
Compared to her, they are mild.

Telepathically is how we speak,
Even across the wildest creek.

Though she may not be here,
With God looking after her, I have no fear.

Here is wishing you a happy life,
Attain God's knowledge is what you must strive.

My sister respects you so greatly, O Ganesha!
Knowing you represent *Ishwara*.

# Shoot The Goal

First you got to shoot the goal,
Then the mystery you can begin to unfold.

So opposite to anything I play,
The holy cow and me molded by clay.

The essence is in everything,
The birds to fly you have given the wing.

When with you this ceases to exist,
Material temptations; difficult to resist.

Your breath is the vehicle; pay attention,
Focus between your eyebrows with intense concentration,
Then will come a deadly confrontation.

Implode into the point of light,
To merge with God is your birthright.

Your religion and country are part of your ego,
For God the truth, even that one must let go.

Spread knowledge of the Light is what I must,
Soon I will be just dust.

# **Magic**

It's not really day, it's not really night,
It's in between, it's called the twilight.

From the sea to the sky lo!
If it's not a tsunami, it's a tornado.

Miracles are a daily show,
Like Lord Ram stringing the invincible bow.

Mind blowing are the sounds, colours, shapes you create,
An artist can only try to imitate.

Either you can see the magic,
Or, your life is indeed tragic.

*(Note: In the Merchant Navy, I encountered a tsunami and many Tropical Revolving Storms)*

# **Trance**

Most around me live in a trance,
Having no idea of your cosmic dance.

When does everyone get to know you?
Why reveal yourself only to a few?

It causes me so much pain,
When I talk of you all in vain.

In the middle of the ocean, in nowhere,
You showed me your presence everywhere.

Absolute delight and utter confusion,
From the moment of our fusion.

Countless in front are your entities,
Each having an individual identity.

You are made of such fine light, love tissue,
No beginning, no end, an ageless issue.

At times I feel like a master,
Then, on the other hand, an utter disaster.

# Mom

With patience she has brought me up,
So much love, it keeps overflowing the cup.

She comforts me when I am in pain,
Or else a long time ago, I would have gone insane.

I get scolded when she is right,
Rarely has she misused her might.

I love you mom beyond compare,
When you need me I will be there.

God is here in a disguise for me,
The faster I realise, the better things shall be.

## **Tree**

Now it is time for spring,
The leaves will take wings.

This beautiful tree is going to become dry,
Preparing for a new set on to try.

She will then don a shining new Armor,
Her beauty you will want to devour.

How long has this been going on?
From her too, life one day will be torn.

Each is somehow doing their part,
All in your endless art.

# What

When the truth is mocked,
How sad it is to be flocked.

The cunning minds of the people we care,
How they hit us here and there.

This tree I see standing in front of me,
How much more confusion can there be?

What are these clouds in the sky?
Am I to believe I can fly?

Am I bound to become a wanderer?
Or am I meant to stand here forever?

When my time is immediately near,
I hope I can show no fear.

I know I have done so in the past,
What was I doing during that play's cast?

The turbulent mind, if it doesn't have a reason to die,
Will very slowly and surely fry.

Drinking tea has become a hobby for me,
It gives me time to pause and think of eternity.

What we have been taught is so full of rot,
Such beauty lies when it is all shot.

Whatever you do try your best,
Unto God leave the rest.

# Charity

Thoughts of hunger,
Inside erupts anger.

So much is there for all of us,
One man hoards and creates the fuss.

Security I can understand,
But generosity must go hand in hand.

Taking was so easy, no accountability,
In giving there is strength, courage and responsibility.

God guides us all the time,
In not paying attention there will be a fine.

When I know something is right,
Then with prayer and faith I must fight,
God is behind me with all His might.

We all belong to Him,
The word coincidence is the foolish man's whim.

These lessons are for us to grow,
The bark of the tree was in one essence
made for the crow.

# Peace

Everybody is acting busy,
The mind inward uneasy.

One victory followed by a downfall,
To start again till nightfall.

Peace with all brings tranquility,
Mind altering reality.

These wars justified or are they lame?
It's with love and not terror that One gets tamed.

# Win Some Lose Some

Trust only in God,
Faithful then comes the dog.

The human is a racist,
Indeed also, a sadist.

You seem to enjoy it when I burn,
Why should I show remorse when it is your turn?

By so many I have been deceived,
Of course, I am peeved.

More so at myself,
The other was the cause itself.

To love is to respect and trust,
Something so often is unjust.

Either you think divine,
Or, you think like a swine.

You win some, you lose some,
Decide wisely for the outcome.

# God Knows

This pen has a cap on it,
Or else, the nib will disintegrate.

Some people are so kind to you,
The reality is there are quite a few.

Orange, yellow, green all the colours in front,
Three dimension life so often looks blunt.

I feel like I am the centre of the world,
Then on someone's little finger
I feel I am being twirled.

The glasses on an old man,
He is soon to go where he won't need the fan.

What unbelievable creativity,
You are always in activity.

How are you creating? Is what I want to know,
That is the only way I can grow.

Secrets, mysteries of the past,
Some seem so eternally to last.

# Dream

Summer is over and winter has come,
It seems like an endless mathematical sum.

Sage Aryabhata an enlightened adept,
Invented Zero, such a crazy concept.

Everything is so much in abundance,
Why is there in me such reluctance?

Dream on … dream on … don't stop,
Try living your dreams or become a flop.

Where in the world are your dreams coming from?
There seems to be no stop ever since I was born.

Some dreams have become a reality,
Some seem to end in utter futility.

What is this thing we call sixth sense?
It is made so that at times you can cross the fence.

At times, I am filled with such joy,
At times, such sadness; like a child breaking his toy.

Where am I supposed to go from here?
Confront I must, my deepest fear.

# Alone

I think it is best to be alone,
Then life you will not bemoan.

You are totality,
With someone else you lose your vitality.

So many have come and gone,
Both lost and none won.

Then I start all over again,
This cat and mouse game of blame.

Where does all this lead?
Bit by bit I slowly bleed.

So important becomes the money,
Without which, no toast or honey.

I found you so horrible yesterday,
I wonder what I feel for you today.

I wish I could retrace my steps and erase my track,
Now I am even more determined to never come back.

Detach, detach, detach.

# Once Again

I have forgotten her so completely,
Or, was she really part of my history?

The past seems to have such a long shadow,
This world is filled with so much sorrow.

This is one weird dimension,
At the end will be my redemption.

I am hopeless, I keep falling in love,
Hoping this time her hand will fit the glove.

Sometimes, I feel I will never learn,
From the mistakes I made,
when I crashed on my last turn.

As much as I laugh, I must cry,
Simple rules of this game before I die.

# Gone Mad

Some say I am an idiot,
Some say I am a total nut.

Some say I am lazy,
Some say I am crazy.

I care and I really don't care what they say,
Patiently accepting what comes my way.

I know I am going to die soon,
That will be my biggest boon.

My life like a candle has been lit,
Suicide sadly is forbidden to commit.

Fool make money, some people shout,
Poetry! you will die broke without a doubt.

I must write, I keep telling them,
I have been given the signs to use the pen.

# **Intoxication**

At times, I love getting intoxicated,
When happy or irritated.

Sometimes, I become so relaxed,
Or else, I get doubly taxed.

Too much intoxication can drive you mad,
People will look and say so sad.

I must have fallen in love twenty times that night,
Now, I am sober it sure gives me a fright.

I was not born an alcoholic or such,
I just like that drink so much.

Beware a little too much can become a bane,
All your goodwill, good work can go down the drain.

# Married To The Light

One angry word or sentence from my lover,
And life seems to end forever.

Then she smiles and teases me,
Sure as hell it pleases me.

I must die and she must too,
What is it together we should do?

I dream of her night and day,
The cosmos having made it this way.

The light being her reality,
Eventually, to be united in eternity.

A tear in her eye,
The world deserves to die.

True love is only with God when we pray,
But then, God is in every man or woman they say.

I know I am married to the light,
Should I find a partner for my earthly delight?

# Infinity

God and religion is so complicated,
So when you talk of it, some people get irritated.

It simply means the dimension of death,
In all aspects, takes away your breath.

The moment you submit to the point of light,
The word death is no more such a fright.

Infinity you become at once,
The human form you then trounce.

That's when you realise everything is alive,
The wind, the rain, even the nectar of the beehive.

The endless darkness in front of us all,
Is as alive as the closest insect to crawl.

When in love with one of your form,
It is a retreat in the storm.

What to do at the next bend?
Maybe things will come to an end.

Till then, should I follow my heart as you order?
Or, let my life be in disorder?

## My Second Father
## – Dr. Naozer Kavarana

I got so much love from this great man,
Not once in my life from him I ran.

A doctor by profession is what he was,
Following a noble cause.

So vast was his knowledge indeed,
But about death not much did he heed.

Then death came to him at last,
A clean slate he had to make of his past.

He signed some papers with a trembling hand,
Aware he was going to leave this land.

The responsibilities that he had to fulfill,
Humorously coping with the last pill.

One more day is left for me,
Then home to eternity.

'Follow your star', he told his son,
'You too my child must become one.'

# Anil Prem Sharma

In order to know your perfection,
You keep playing with my heart's affection.

Now a friend you have taken,
Once again my heart you have broken.

You are the One who gave him birth,
His soul I pray is with you,
As his body is with Mother Earth.

# **Confusion**

Life is circles in circles inside out,
Just forever keeps me in doubt.

I chase something it just goes away,
Nothing is meant forever to stay.

Then I say forget it, let me be free,
Out of nowhere it is right in front of me.

Confusion in life belongs to us all,
It's something I wish with time I could stall.

Some are so beautiful, some so repulsive,
I feel like sticking to some like adhesive.

The waiter works so hard all day,
How is he content with such a miserable pay?

The boss needs to have a broad shoulder,
The stress at times is like carrying a heavy boulder.

# Sameer S. Shetty

Sameer (*anna*) my childhood friend,
All this, one day will end.

A smart human anyone can tell,
God fearing, he is sure to go to heaven from this hell.

A lovely sense of humor,
He speaks so well and doesn't murmur.

We have had; many a great times,
In life, I am sure he will shine.

Sameer (*anna*) my childhood friend,
All this one day will end.

# God

Who is God?
He, she and it is God. God is, has, was, will.

Where is God?
Everywhere is God, nowhere is God.

What sort of a thing is God?
Everything is God.
God is Love, God is the Light.

When does God come?
When the madness stops, when death becomes.

How do I see God?
With your eyes closed and with your eyes open.

What have I to do with God?
You are his creation, you are a part of him.

When do I see, meet God?
Whenever you really decide to,
When you want nothing.

# The Ultimate Plan

The ultimate plan,
I just don't understand.

We are all somehow put together,
Particles of dust, water, vacuum and ether.

That bulb in the sky is termed as a star,
Seems so close but alas is so far.

The moth dangling on the ceiling,
I wonder, what is she feeling?

Trillions and trillions of pieces perfectly in place,
Which includes the human race.

# The Now

Living in the now is being one with God,
Or else, one is just a fraud.

Live for now and plan for tomorrow,
Otherwise, expect sorrow.

My dreams are my job,
There none can rob.

People who claim to be practical,
Lost souls indeed theatrical.

All your practicalities will cease to exist,
The moment death you cease to resist.

# Lady

She is so gorgeous,
Seeing her with someone else makes me jealous.

A stunning piece of art,
I wouldn't like to see her depart.

How do I approach her?
In me, there is a fear.

Mystical creatures in your majestic play,
Nothing is meant forever to stay.

Love starts through the eyes,
My soul with joy cries.

What Albert Einstein termed optical delusion,
The Indians termed *Maya* or illusion.

# **Tossed**

Each in his own world,
Here and there, is tossed and twirled.

At which age I wonder, I am going to die,
Dream stage to awakened; one must try.

So difficult to concentrate on one point,
The way for the soul and super soul to get joint.

Back to the past and into the future,
This mad mind one needs to nurture.

# Eternity

My friends are yellow, brown and white,
What difference does it make to the light?

The joke that beholds us all,
Comes to us only at the moment of our greatest fall.

Death is our friend,
Where there is no trend,
Why fear? It is really near.

Why show me the light? Why confuse me?
Ignorance was bliss, why did you diffuse me?

To know is to be a liar,
What better way to throw me into fire?

When in pain I say your name,
The reality that is, is no more the same.

The light that shines beyond the stars,
Is the same in all our hearts.

# Life

Money is also a part of God,
Don't earn it by committing a fraud.

The haunting moments of the past,
You need to drop in order to last.

What happened was for the good of all,
Only by letting go, you stand tall.

Getting hurt is a part and parcel of life,
It just makes you stronger so that you can survive.

If it is due, it will come to you,
Stop being jealous of the few.

Try you must that's for sure,
Burn away desires, your soul's cure.

Everyone is placed in a certain situation,
Inevitable is also the transition.

Life and death both must come,
It is said at the end, we become One.

# The Master

The Buddha sits in serenity,
Quietly observing eternity.

I am so clamored by material thoughts,
So many things, I wish I had bought.

The Masters have such a majestic smile,
Something I permanently file.

I get angry so often and I ask: Why me?
He says, 'Patience is needed in order to see.'

The future is something I bother about,
It just keeps filling me with so much doubt.

The light at the end of the tunnel I know is there,
It's so difficult to be aware.

Keep going is something I have to do,
The Fruit may come for me to chew.

Humble I must be till I last,
Not forgetting my painful past.

Everything in life is different today,
Nothing is there forever to stay.

Pain and happiness, I must appreciate,
They lead to the eternal gate.

# Desperate For Attention

Some people are so desperate for attention,
They try to get it at the cost of your cremation.

Why can't they remain humble and free?
They pull you down in front of the world to see.

They don't look so good and are not too amusing,
An insult from them is not bemusing.

The magic in them is so clear,
It all goes when they show such fear.

They are fooling themselves is what it is,
Never mind it is all going to end in bliss.

Make peace with yourself is what they say,
I have my friend when will you do, I pray.

These desperate acts are so embarrassing,
Do you understand the word called harassing?

The seeds in the garden someday must grow,
Everything is alright is what I want you to know.

# Do Right

I hope I do the right thing,
Then happiness to all I will bring.

How do I make people understand?
We are all part of the same band.

Fight you can when you are right,
But never unnecessarily abuse your might.

Dawn is here and the night will start,
Day will come and the night will have to part.

This seems to go on forever,
Just like a mighty river.

The binding force is love,
The symbol being a white dove.

# Focus

You have the palms and you have the date,
Incomprehensible, how all things have been made.

Children make me so happy,
Adults, intolerable and snappy.

Who is the foreigner? Who is the alien?
We are one in your plain.

What exactly is my purpose?
Right now, I am unsure where to focus.

Time, at times, seems to move so slow,
All in you, we agelessly flow.

In unity there is more strength,
Foolish wars, we can then prevent.

He is fighting basically for the land,
Thinking he would have the upper hand.

Momentarily, he may be overjoyed,
Then in sadness, he will be employed.

# Curiosity

It has to start with curiosity,
Only to fathom the absurdity.

Man feels foolishly strong,
When to others he does wrong.

What's going to be my next surprise?
Into all before I vaporise.

Most around are so lonely,
Content are some on being homely.

The second hand is ticking by,
Time so often has made me cry.

My body aches, I need a massage,
How much will he or she charge?

# Ungrateful

Knowing you are perfect,
I still curse you with disrespect.

I am sorry for being ungrateful,
You so often spoil me, you are playful.

I need to remember I am insipid,
How can you harm me, my beautiful cupid?

When will you teach me your arts?
My soul foolishly from here to there, darts.

# Youth

I would race you till there was so much fun,
As a child how much did I run.

The word 'ice-cream' brought me such joy,
Hoping it would come and was not a wicked ploy.

To play was about all I wanted,
Geometry I loved, the only subject I took for granted.

Basketball, table tennis, football was all I looked forward to,
The classes; dreadful- something I had to do.

History dates, chemistry formula
bounced over my head,
If I didn't memorise them, I would be dead.

I learned to think, read and write,
Examinations getting close would bring me a fright.

The best part was the friends I made,
Some have lasted for many a decade.

# The Human

So often I feel the need to possess,
It is a situation I need to reassess.

Nothing really belongs to me,
At the same time, all is mine as far as I can see.

Different situations I have gone through with time,
Deep down all is fine.

This human nature makes me complain,
Sometimes, I feel like getting out,
By just taking the next plane or train.

Some say he is running away from life,
Rubbish I say, wherever he goes he needs to survive.

Let's try and stop putting other people down,
It only gives us a foolish reason to frown.

It's all you, is what you need to comprehend,
That's when some foolish laws can be bent.

Everything has been made just for you,
And not only for a few.

Love is the door to God,
A funny thing, as it can never get you bored.

# **Trespassing**

Sometimes life goes into the beyond,
If only, I could be forewarned.

To love someone so totally,
At times seems such a frivolity.

Love is like a yo-yo,
From heaven to hell to and fro.

How long do you plan to keep me here?
Tormented and in constant fear.

What am I supposed to do? Is so confusing,
I feel on earth, I am trespassing.

So often, I ask you to show me a sign,
Thus, I remember you as divine.

You constantly look after me,
That is why, I am drinking this tea.

Some say I will live till forty,
Then home, I will come to your endless beauty.

# Strange

These lights, these stars so far away,
All I know is we call it the Milky Way.

Everything around, is so strange,
The human is certainly deranged.

Success is peace of mind,
I try so hard to unwind.

We care constantly; fighting like cats and dogs,
Reality is covered by some strange fog.

How long is this supposed to go on?
Before I go back to where I came from.

In this world, we are all referring,
To sparks of happiness and flames of suffering.

The wise are so totally detached,
Pain is for those who are attached.

# Death

Death comes to you in the middle of the night,
Or, sweeps you away in broad daylight.

This being man's biggest doubt,
Death is not to be talked about.

Where he comes from, where he goes?
We have no tangible proof that shows.

The masters say there is a holy light,
In the beginning and during our last flight.

How do I overcome my fear of death?
By leading a good life and having no regrets.

The moment I die I must do my best,
To become one with the light, eternal rest.

The soul must merge with the super-soul,
Forever to become part of the whole.

As long as I have much to give,
That is how long I will live.

At the end; to death I must go,
Finishing a real tragic and funny show.

# Glossary

*Maya* – Hindu Term for illusion.

*Ishwara* – Hindu Term for God.

Tsunami – Japanese name for tidal wave.

Death Point – Buddhist definition for your last breath.

*Santhara* – Jain tradition where a terminally ill person or someone who believes he has accomplished his purpose on the planet voluntarily undergoes a fast unto death in order to merge with God.

*Samadhi* – Hindu term signifying a state of union with God, same as enlightenment.

*Aghora* – A Hindu sect, worshippers of Shiva.

Shamanism – Belief and practice regarding the spiritual world, shaman being the practitioner.

"The only way you can conquer me is through love and there I am gladly conquered."

— Krishna

# About the author

Born in 1970 in Mumbai to a Hindu father and Parsee mother. Studied in Cathdral and John Connon then Jaihind College before joining the Merchant Navy. Graduated from LBS Nauitical college and worked as a Second Mate or Navigating Officer in the Merchant Navy for around 7 years.

A spiritual Experience in the middle of the Atlantic Ocean altered his course of life and he was given signs to share God knowledge via the medium of poetry. He started writing at the age of 30 and at the age of 33 he left everything to become a full time poet and lived in a basement temple dedicated to Shirdi Sai Baba in Pune India for around two years. He spend a total of 11 years working on his book Ponder Awhile before he was satisfied with it. He is currently 53 years old.